QED
Word Banks

ZEEBO'S
Numbers

Wendy Body

QED Publishing

QED

QED
Word Banks

ZEEBO'S
Numbers

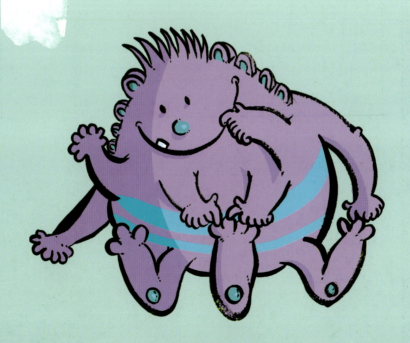

A Catalogue record for this book is available from the British Library.

ISBN 1 84538 459 8

Written by Wendy Body
Designed by Alix Wood
Editor Hannah Ray
Illustrated by Sanja Rescek

Series Consultant Anne Faundez
Publisher Steve Evans
Creative Director Louise Morley
Editorial Manager Jean Coppendale

Printed and bound in China

My name is Zeebo and
I'm **five** not **two**,
I'm a marvellous monster
but do I look like you?

I've got **legs** and **knees**, I've got **fingers** too,
I've got **six** stretchy **arms**, and that's more
arms than you!

1 one · 2 two · 3 three · 4 four · 5 five

finger

arm

knee

leg

6 six · 7 seven · 8 eight · 9 nine · 10 ten

7

I've got **four** small **ears** each side of my head,
I've got **two eyes** that shut when I'm sleeping
in bed.

1 one 2 two 3 three 4 four 5 five

ear

eye

6 six 7 seven 8 eight 9 nine 10 ten

9

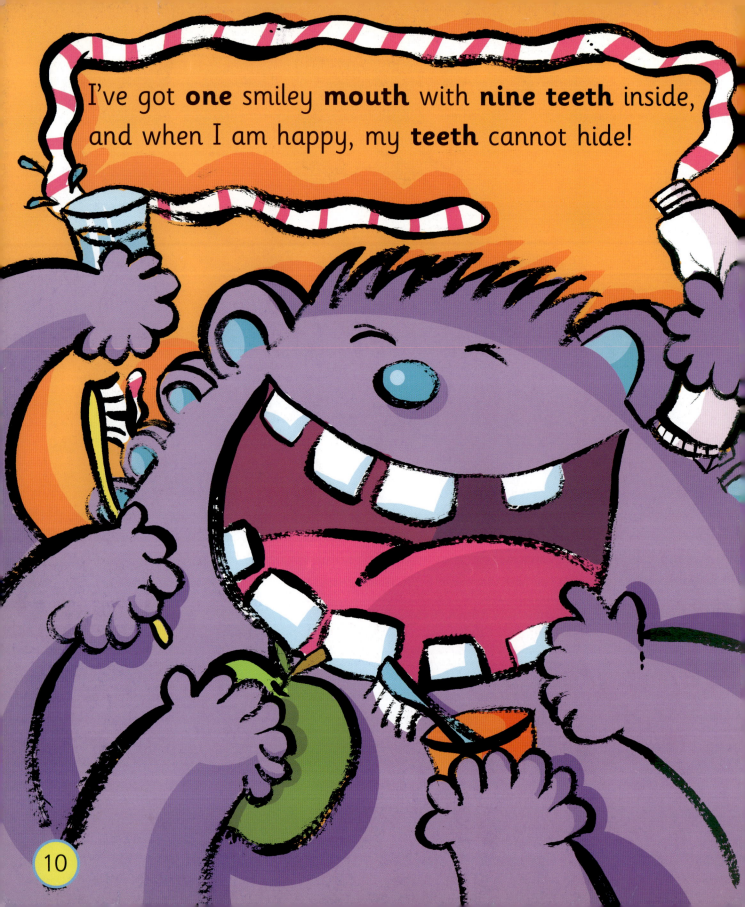

I've got **one** smiley **mouth** with **nine teeth** inside, and when I am happy, my **teeth** cannot hide!

1 one　2 two　3 three　4 four　5 five

mouth

tooth

6 six　7 seven　8 eight　9 nine　10 ten

I've got **hair** that's like my father's and mother's, each **one** of my **eight hairs** looks just like the others.

1 one 2 two 3 three 4 four 5 five

hair

6 six 7 seven 8 eight 9 nine 10 ten

13

With the **seven fingers** I've got on each **hand**,
I can play the piano in our Monster band.

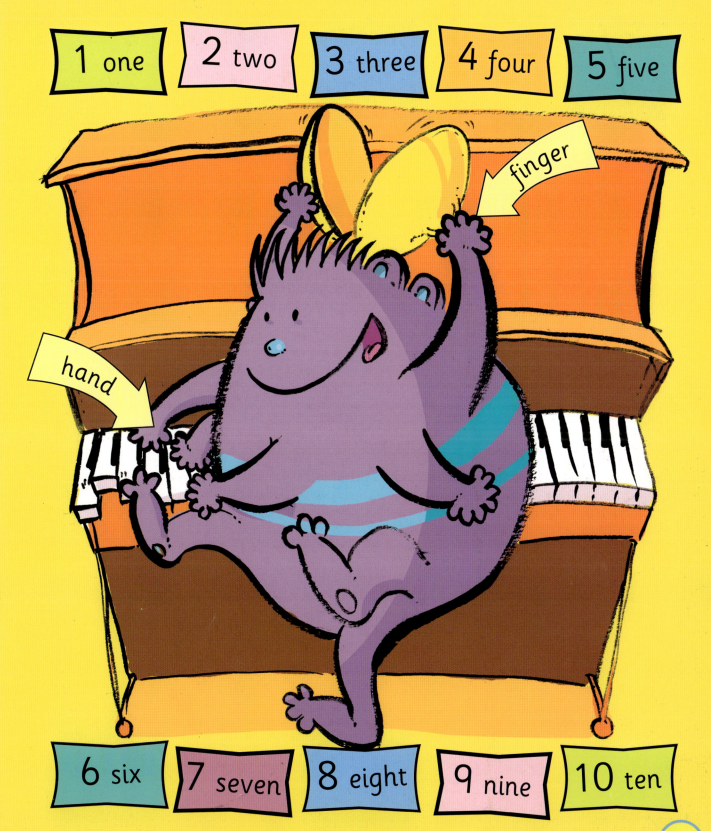

1 one 2 two 3 three 4 four 5 five

finger

hand

6 six 7 seven 8 eight 9 nine 10 ten

15

I've got **three** short **legs** and **three** little **feet**
to jump, skip and dance to our rock and roll beat!

1 one   2 two   3 three   4 four   5 five

leg

foot

6 six   7 seven   8 eight   9 nine   10 ten

I feel a bit sad I've got only **one nose**,
so I make myself laugh by counting my **toes**:
one, **two**, **three**, **four**, **five**, **six**, **seven**, **eight**,
nine, **TEN**!

Word bank

Words from the story

1 one
2 two
3 three
4 four
5 five
6 six
7 seven
8 eight
9 nine
10 ten

More words

11 eleven
12 twelve
13 thirteen
14 fourteen
15 fifteen
16 sixteen
17 seventeen
18 eighteen
19 nineteen
20 twenty

What do you notice about these words?

Parents' and teachers' notes

- As you read the book to your child, run your finger along underneath the text. This will help your child to follow the reading and focus on the look of the words, as well as their sound.

- Once your child is familiar with the book, encourage him or her to join in with the reading.

- Help your child to both see and understand the illustrations. Use open-ended questions to encourage your child to respond, e.g. 'What's happening on this page?'

- Encourage your child to express opinions and preferences. Ask questions such as, 'Which picture do you think is the funniest? Why?'

- Ask your child to make comparisons between Zeebo and himself or herself. Ask questions such as, 'How old is Zeebo?' 'Is that older or younger than you?'

- Discuss Zeebo's appearance. Encourage your child to invent and describe a monster of his or her own. Make a labelled picture of the monster and give the monster a name.

- Draw your child's attention to the structure of some words, e.g. the plural form 'feet' in the text and singular 'foot' in the label. Look at the construction of some of the words, e.g. 'Eight'. Explain that 'eight' is a tricky word. It sounds like it has only two letters, ay-t, but actually it has five.

- Look at the 'Things to do' pages (pages 20–21). Read the instructions/questions to your child and help him or her with the answers where necessary. Give your child lots of praise and encouragement. Even if he or she gets something wrong, you can say: 'That was a really good try, but it's not that one it's this one.'

- Together, read and discuss the words on the 'Word bank' pages (pages 22–23). Look at the letter patterns and how the different words are spelled. Cover up the first part of a word and see if your child can remember what was there. See if your child can write the simpler words from memory — he or she is likely to need several attempts to write a word correctly!

- When you are talking about letter sounds, try not to add too much of an uh or er sound. Say mmm instead of muh or mer, ssss instead of suh or ser. Saying letter sounds as carefully as possible will help your child when he or she is trying to build up or spell words — ler-e-ger doesn't sound much like 'leg'!

- Talk about words: what they mean, how they sound, how they look and how they are spelled; but if your child gets restless, or bored, stop. Enjoyment of the story, activity or book is essential if we want children to grow up valuing books and reading!